my first
ROCK PAINTING
BOOK

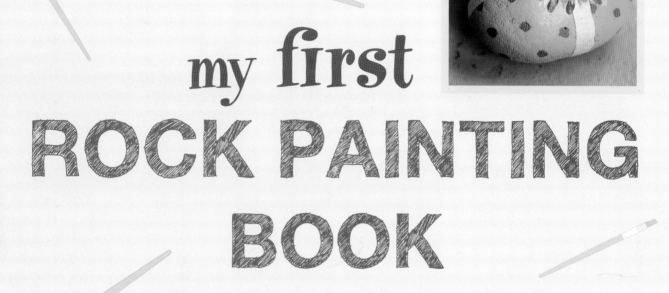

my first
ROCK PAINTING
BOOK

35 fun craft projects for children aged 7+

EMMA HARDY

CICO **Kidz**

Published in 2018 by CICO Kidz

An imprint of Ryland Peters & Small Ltd

20–21 Jockey's Fields   341 E 116th St

London WC1R 4BW   New York, NY 10029

www.rylandpeters.com

10 9 8 7 6 5 4 3 2 1

Text copyright © Emma Hardy 2018

Design, photography, and illustration copyright
© CICO Books 2018

A CIP catalog record for this book is available from the
Library of Congress and the British Library.

ISBN: 978-1-78249-609-0

Printed in China

Series consultant: Susan Akass
Editor: Clare Sayer
Designer: Alison Fenton
Photographer: Debbie Patterson
Step artworks: Rachel Boulton
Animal artworks: Hannah George

In-house editor: Dawn Bates
Art director: Sally Powell
Production controller: Mai-Ling Collyer
Publishing manager: Penny Craig
Publisher: Cindy Richards

Contents

Introduction

Everyone loves the feel of a smooth, rounded pebble in their pocket. But a rock collection can turn into so much more when you begin to paint the rocks. In *My First Rock Painting Book* there are 35 projects to inspire you to get painting.

Whether you are decorating rocks for yourself or to give as gifts, it won't be long before you catch the rock-painting bug and start seeing every pebble and stone as a potential project! Use them as paperweights, fridge magnets, toys, or just eye-catching decorations for your home.

The projects range from simple googly-eyed monsters and pretty painted spots and stripes— perfect to get you started—to more detailed projects like the sushi and Russian dolls, which are perfect to try once you have practiced your painting skills! Each project is graded with one, two, or three smiley faces (see below) so that you can decide easily which ones suit you best. There is a handy materials list, which offers advice on a basic craft kit. You won't need everything on it to get started but it is worth reading before you get going. The techniques section offers tips and advice on painting rocks, which will help you to get the best results.

There are lots of ideas in this book to get you painting, whether you follow the step-by-step instructions exactly or use them as starting blocks for your own designs. I hope that you enjoy rock painting and use your creativity and imagination to make a whole host of fantastic projects!

Project levels

Level 1
These have only a few stages and very simple designs.

Level 2
These include more stages and may require you to mix your own paint colors.

Level 3
These are longer and may have fine details that need a steady hand!

Materials

One of the great things about rock painting is that you need very few materials. Find a nice, smooth stone or pebble, get out some brightly colored paints, choose a design, and then get painting!

Collecting stones and pebbles

Before starting a rock-painting project, you will need stones or pebbles and finding the right ones can be half the fun. Choose those with a smooth surface as they will be easier to paint evenly. Look for particular shapes if you have a project in mind or choose flattish, smooth ones that will be suitable for lots of designs.

Be aware that it is often illegal to take stones from beaches and national parks so check whether you are in a protected area before you take any home. Why not try looking for pebbles and stones in your garden? If you can't collect your own, garden centers, DIY stores, and craft stores usually sell a range of stones and pebbles quite cheaply.

Pens

Pens are useful for outlining painted shapes and for adding more detail. Felt-tipped pens will work on painted stones, although they can sometimes smudge and the lines may not stand out very well. Fine liners and marker pens can add strong lines and are easy to use on stones.

Glue

Some of the projects in this book require stones to be stuck together. The best glue to use is fast-drying PVA/craft glue. There are several different makes available so have a look in your local craft store. Hot glue guns can also be used, although you will need to ask an adult to help you with these.

Paints

The projects in this book all use acrylic paints as they are more permanent and perfect for painting stones. However, beginners may prefer to use water-based poster paints as you can easily wash off any mistakes you make and have another go. If you get any on your clothes, it will wash out. A basic set of red, blue, yellow, green, purple, black, and white can be mixed to create a whole range of beautiful colors.

Paintbrushes

It is a good idea to have a range of paintbrushes in different sizes. Use wider ones to paint whole stones and smaller and finer ones for adding details. Make sure that you look after your paintbrushes so that they will last a long time. Always wash them after using them by rinsing them under a running cold faucet (tap) until the water runs clear. Leave them to dry somewhere flat so that the bristles dry smooth.

Varnish

Painted stones do not need to be varnished, but applying a coat of varnish will protect the paint. This is useful if you are making stones into toys that will be played with a lot. It can also give the stones a slightly glossy look. Use a water-based varnish, which you can buy from craft stores, although you can also use PVA/craft glue that has been diluted with an equal amount of water.

Other useful things

Apron—protect your clothes whenever you paint by wearing an apron or a big old T-shirt over the top.

Pencil—useful for drawing your design onto a stone before painting it.

Scrap paper—painting stones can be a messy business so always make sure that the table or surface that you are working on is covered in scrap paper or newspaper to protect it.

Pot for water—needed for cleaning your brushes. An old jar or plastic food tub will work well for this. Change your water as soon as it gets dirty to stop the paint looking muddy.

Old rag—useful for drying paintbrushes after cleaning so you can re-use with another paint color.

Mixing palette or white plate—perfect for mixing paints on, although you can also use a disposable paper plate.

Modeling clay—useful for holding stones in place while they are being glued together.

Egg cups or small pots—use these to stand your stones in while they dry.

Things to stick on stones—googly eyes, buttons, and beads can all be used to decorate your stones. Glitter works well on painted stones, too. Stickers can add a fun touch, either using them as decoration or sticking them onto a stone, painting over them, and then removing them to leave a pattern (see Stars and Stripes on page 84). Small magnets can be bought in craft stores and can simply be glued on to the backs of pebbles to turn stones into fridge magnets.

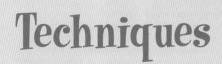

Techniques

Most of the projects in this book have really simple designs and very few techniques. However, there are a few things to know to make sure you get great results every time, from preparing your pebbles, to blending paint colors and adding fine details.

Cleaning pebbles

Make sure that your stones and pebbles are clean before you start painting. Wash them with warm, soapy water and dry with a clean cloth. If your stone feels gritty, an old toothbrush can be handy. Simply brush it over the surface of the stone to remove any sand or dirt.

Drawing your design on the stone

You may find it useful to draw your design onto the stone before painting. Paint the base coat on to the stone and leave to dry before drawing or draw straight on to the stone using a pencil to give you lines to paint inside.

Painting

• Lots of the projects in this book need a base coat of paint. Either use the color needed for your design or paint with a coat of white paint, which can help the colors to look brighter. Paint one side of the stone, leave to dry, and then paint the other side so the whole stone is covered.

• You will be able to mix lots of colors of paint with your basic kit (see page 8). Experiment by mixing a few colors together or adding white paint to lighten the color or a little black paint to make it darker.

• Always leave paint to dry before adding more layers or more details. Acrylic paint dries quickly so you shouldn't have to wait long. Ask an adult if you can use a hairdryer to speed up the process or leave the painted stone somewhere warm for a few minutes.

• Some pebbles are painted in bold, solid colors. Other projects need to have paint colors blended together. To do this, paint stripes or patches of the colors that you are using onto the pebble and then, while the paint is still wet, use a clean, dry paintbrush to brush over the paints and blend them together so that the colors merge.

• Lots of the designs use dots or small circles. You can use a paintbrush to make these but an easy way to make even-sized dots is to dip a Q-tip (cotton bud) into some paint and then just "dot" it onto your pebble.

Adding details with pen

For fiddly details, a black pen is perfect. Make sure that the paint is completely dry before you start and carefully draw onto the stone. Be careful not to smudge the ink before it has a chance to dry, although any smudges or mistakes can easily be painted over.

Gluing pebbles together

Gluing pebbles together can create some fun 3D designs. Paint the pebbles first and when they are dry, glue them together, holding them in place with small pieces of modeling clay until the glue is dry.

Varnishing

Before you varnish your painted stones, it is a good idea to try out the varnish on a small patch of your painted stone to make sure that the varnish will not smudge the paint. Once you have done this, apply a coat of varnish or watered-down PVA/craft glue (see page 8) using a dry brush. Leave it to dry completely before touching it.

SAFETY FIRST!
Never give small painted pebbles to young children, especially those that look like food, as they may swallow them.

chapter 1

Fabulous Food

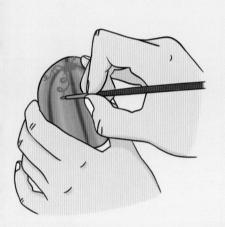

Striped candies

Fill a jar with these pretty pebble candies in pastel colors. Make a few of each kind so it looks like a mix of different flavors.

You will need

Small round and oval-shaped pebbles

White acrylic paint

Acrylic paint in colors of your choice, such as black, red, pink, yellow, orange, purple, and blue

Mixing palette or white plate

Medium and fine paintbrushes

1 Using a medium paintbrush, paint each pebble with a white base coat. The whole pebble needs to be painted, not just the front, so paint one half of each pebble, leave it to dry, and then paint the other side. Leave the pebbles to dry completely.

2 Decide what colors you want your candies to be and mix up some pale shades by blending colors with white paint. Leave some of the pebbles white and paint others in pale pink, yellow, blue, and green. You need to make sure you cover the whole pebble, so paint one side first, as in Step 1.

3 With a fine paintbrush, paint stripes in darker shades on the oval pebbles, working from end to end on one side. Leave them to dry, then turn the pebbles over and paint more stripes, joining them up with those on the other side if you wish.

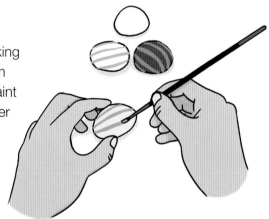

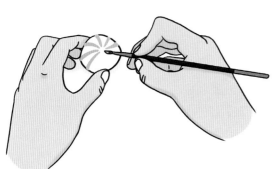

Warning: Remember that they may look like sweets, but these candy pebbles must never be put in your mouth. Never give them to young children.

4 Paint stripes on the flat round pebbles but this time start near the center on the front and paint stripes out to the edges all the way round. Leave to dry, then turn over and paint the same design on the other side, matching up the ends of the stripes as if they go right round.

Tip

Varnishing the painted pebbles (see page 8) will make the paint finish a bit tougher and give them a lovely, glossy sheen. Make sure the painted pebbles are completely dry first.

Tiny fruit

Once you've made a few trays of these fruit pebbles you'll be able to set up your own farmers' market stall! Collect little boxes and baskets whenever you see them to use for your fruit, or you could make some from cardboard.

You will need

Tiny fruit-shaped pebbles

Acrylic paints in the following colors: green, yellow, orange, white, black, red, and purple

Medium and fine paintbrushes

Black fine liner

Tiny boxes or baskets

A little hay or dried grass

1 Using a medium paintbrush, paint the pebbles orange for the oranges, yellow for the lemons and bunches of bananas, green for the apples, and lighter green (add some white paint to the green) for the pears, pale purple (mix some white paint to the purple paint) for grapes, and red for the strawberries. Try to paint the whole pebble (it can get messy!). Paint up to nine of each color depending on the size of your containers. Leave them all to dry.

2 For the apples, paint a smudge of red paint on each apple to give them a rosy blush.

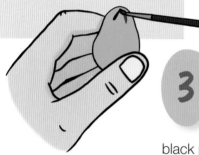

3 Using a fine paintbrush, paint a small stalk and leaf on each one of the apples and pears with brown and dark green paint (add a little black paint to the green paint).

4 For the lemons and limes, paint a green leaf onto each one with a fine paintbrush and add a few dots to each one using the fine liner.

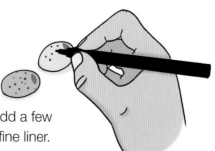

5 For the oranges, draw a little star shape using the fine liner onto each one and paint a few green leaves on to them.

6 For the bananas, draw banana shapes onto the painted yellow pebbles using the fine liner.

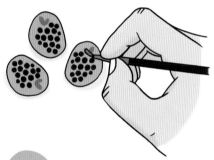

7 For the grapes, use a fine paintbrush to paint small dots onto the pebbles that you painted pale purple using the darker purple paint. Paint a small green stalk onto each one.

8 Paint tiny yellow dots onto the strawberries for the seeds and a dab of green paint to look like a stalk.

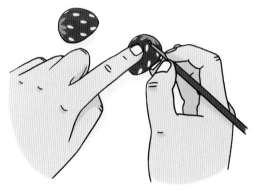

! Warning: This fruit may look tasty, but it must never be put in your mouth. Never give them to small children.

9 Fill the baskets and boxes with hay or dried grass snipped into short lengths. Arrange your fruit on top.

Cakes and buns

Any teddy bears' picnic or dolls' tea party will need cake.
Paint all of your favorites to make perfect cupcakes and
buns that don't need cooking.

You will need

Mixing palette or white plate

Acrylic paint in the following
colors: brown, white, yellow,
red, green, and blue

Medium and fine paintbrushes

Flattish round and oval
pebbles—the shape of
cupcakes and buns

Small round pebbles
for cherries

Fast-drying PVA/craft glue

1 Mix white paint with a little brown paint and a little yellow paint to make the sponge cake color. Paint some of the pebbles with it and leave to dry.

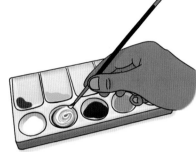

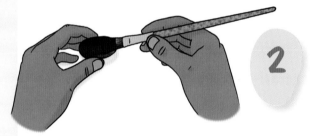

2 Paint a few pebbles in brown paint for the chocolate cakes and leave them to dry.

3 Paint "frosting" onto some of the cakes either with brown paint, white paint, or mix some red paint with white paint to make pink and some blue paint with white paint to make pale blue. It can be quite splodgy so don't worry about straight lines! Leave them all to dry.

4 Paint sprinkles onto some of the cakes using a fine paintbrush, either with small straight lines or dots randomly over the frosting, in brown paint for chocolate sprinkles or in pink, pale blue, yellow, and green for colorful ones.

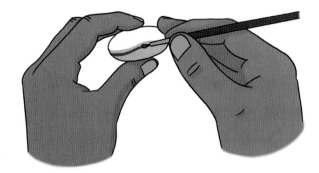

5 Using red paint or white paint, paint a jammy or creamy layer around the middle of some of the cakes. Again, don't worry about it being too neat.

6 To add a cherry onto your cakes, paint the small pebbles with red paint and leave to dry. When the paint has completely dried, glue the cherries onto the tops of the cakes.

Scrummy, yummy CAKES and BUNS!

Super sushi

Japanese sushi are more like tiny works of art than food, which is why it works so well when you paint stones to look like sushi rolls.

You will need

Small pebbles in squarish shapes

Larger, longer-shaped pebbles

Paint in the following colors: white, black, red, yellow, orange, green, and red

Medium and fine paintbrushes

Mixing palette or white plate

1 Start with one of your small square-shaped pebbles. Paint the whole pebble with white paint, leaving one side to dry before turning it over and painting the other side. Leave to dry.

2 Paint a wide band of black round the edge of the pebble to look like sushi seaweed. Leave it to dry.

3 Mix a little black paint with white to make a very light gray. With a fine paintbrush, make small brushstrokes to look like rice all over the top of the pebble in a random pattern— the rougher the better!

4 Now for the filling: use the red, orange, yellow, green, and white paints to mix up some extra colors, such as pink or light green. Paint the vegetable or raw fish part of the sushi, using a few brushstrokes or dots of paint.

Tip

Use the photographs on these pages for reference or look at pictures of sushi online for inspiration.

5 To make the larger sushi, paint the whole stone with white paint and allow to dry. Paint the underside as well.

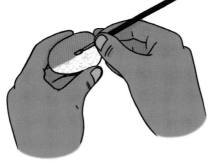

6 Paint the top of the stone with orange paint, mixed with a little white if necessary, to look like salmon.

7 When the orange paint is dry, put a little white paint on a dry paintbrush and brush it over the orange paint in diagonal lines, making about six stripes in total to finish the salmon.

Try picking these up with CHOPSTICKS!

Fantastic fruit

Have fun and use your imagination to find just the right size and shape of pebble for each of your favorite fruits, then paint them in gorgeous colors. We've shown you how to do some but you can think of more—you may even be lucky enough to find a banana-shaped pebble! You'll soon have enough to fill a fruit bowl!

1 Paint a pebble red for the strawberry, green for the pear (mix white paint with dark green to get the right color), red for the watermelon, orange for the satsuma, lime green for the lime, and yellow for the lemon. Paint the two small pebbles red for the cherries. Leave them all to dry.

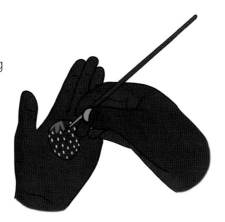

2 For the strawberry, using the fine paintbrush, paint yellow "seeds" all over it using short brush strokes. When they are dry, paint pointy leaves at the top with dark green paint.

You will need

Flat round pebbles for the lemon, lime, satsuma, pear, and strawberry

Flat triangular-shaped pebble for the watermelon slice

2 small round pebbles for the cherries

Acrylic paint in the following colors: red, dark green, white, orange, lime green, yellow, black, and brown

Thick and fine paintbrushes

Mixing palette or white plate

Green chenille stick (pipe cleaner)

Fast-drying PVA/craft glue

Pencil

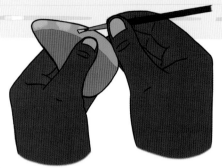

3 For the watermelon, paint the outer edge of the red pebble with a stripe of dark green paint. Leave it to dry completely, then mix a little white paint into the dark green paint to make a lighter green. Paint a few rough stripes, going out toward the edge of the watermelon.

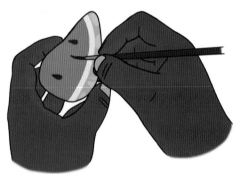

4 When the green paint is dry, use a fine paintbrush to paint a white stripe between the green and the red paint. Now paint three black "seeds" onto the red section.

5 Take the chenille stick (pipe cleaner) and bend it in half. Make a twist about 1¼ in. (3 cm) from the bend to make a leaf shape. Bend the two ends of the chenille stick over a little and then glue them onto the cherry pebbles.

6 For the lemon and limes, paint a white circle a little way from the edge of both of the yellow and lime green pebbles, fill it in with white paint, and leave to dry.

7 With a pencil, mark out triangular segments inside the white circle on both of the pebbles, leaving clear gaps between them. Paint inside the segments in yellow or lime green and then while the paint is still a bit wet, paint a few strokes of the white paint over the top to add a bit of texture.

8 For the pear and satsuma, paint a few spots onto them, in dark green for the pear and in darker orange (add a little bit of red paint to your orange paint) randomly all over the pebbles. Paint a little star shape on the satsuma in the green paint and a stalk in brown paint and a leaf in the green paint on the pear.

Perfect pumpkins

Paint pebbles in the gorgeous orange colors of ripe pumpkins to make a centerpiece for your Halloween party. This is an opportunity to mix different colors and blend them together for a really artistic effect.

You will need

Medium-sized round pebbles

Acrylic paints in the following colors: orange, red, white, and dark green

Mixing palette or white plate

Medium and fine paintbrushes

1 Paint a stone with orange paint and leave to dry. Do not worry about the bottom as this will not show.

2 Mix a little red paint into the orange to make it darker. Using the fine paintbrush, paint lines from the top to the bottom of the stone.

3 On your palette, mix orange paint with a little white, then another blob of orange paint with a bit more white paint, and a third blob with even more white paint to make three shades of orange.

Perfect for HALLOWEEN!

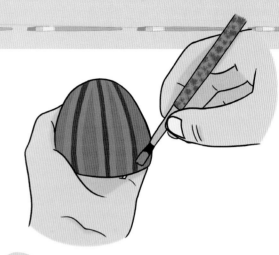

4 Using the medium paintbrush, paint rough stripes of the darker of the three oranges you've just mixed along the edge of the existing stripes. They don't have to be neat and even.

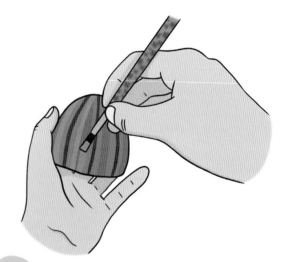

5 Working inward, paint a stripe next to these with the medium orange and one stripe between these with the lightest orange. Again, make them rough and uneven.

6 Working quickly and using a dry paintbrush (any size), brush the colors together to blend them. (See the techniques section on page 10 for more information.)

7 Continue to paint each section in this way.

8 Using green paint, paint the stalk at the top of the pumpkin in a sort of star shape, adding a few curly whirly fronds if you like.

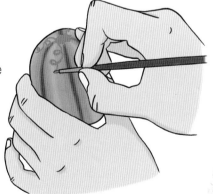

Variation
Pumpkins and squash come in all sorts of lovely colors—use the same technique to paint other squash in shades of red, yellow, and green.

Veggie delights

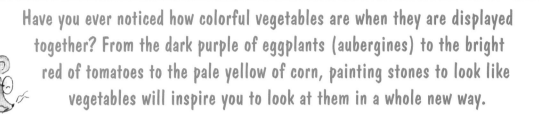

Have you ever noticed how colorful vegetables are when they are displayed together? From the dark purple of eggplants (aubergines) to the bright red of tomatoes to the pale yellow of corn, painting stones to look like vegetables will inspire you to look at them in a whole new way.

You will need

Pebbles in various shapes for a cauliflower, cabbage, eggplant (aubergine), sweetcorn, bell pepper, tomatoes, pea pods, and a potato

Acrylic paints in the following colors: green, white, black, yellow, purple, orange, red, and brown

Mixing palette or white plate

Medium and fine paintbrushes

1 Mix a little yellow paint with white paint to make a very pale yellow and paint the stone for the cauliflower all over. Leave to dry. With green paint, paint the leaves around the edge of the cauliflower, making the tops pointy, and leave to dry.

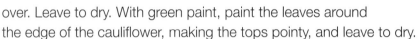

2 Mix a little black paint with some white to make pale gray paint. Using a fine paintbrush, paint some wiggly lines over the yellow part of the cauliflower to look like the florets. This can be quite rough! Leave to dry.

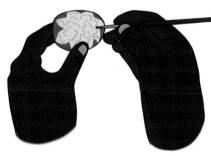

3 Paint the stone for the eggplant (aubergine) purple, the stone for the bell pepper orange, the stone for the cabbage green, the stones for the tomatoes red, and the stone for the potato brown (you can mix a little red, blue, and green paint to make brown, if you wish). Leave them all to dry.

Be inspired to eat your five-a-day!

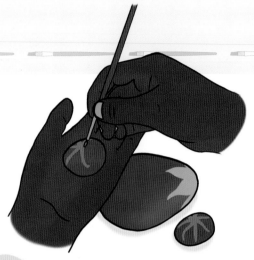

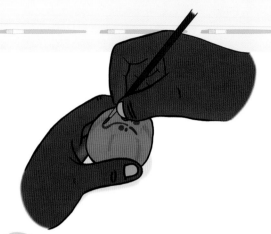

4 Take the eggplant (aubergine) and paint a star shape in green paint on the top of it to look like the stalk. Add a little black paint to the green paint to make it darker and paint the stalks on the tomatoes. They should look like long, pointy stars.

5 Using a slightly darker orange (mix a tiny bit of black into your orange paint), paint a few lines at the top and bottom of the bell pepper stone to look like the curves. Leave to dry, then paint the stalk using dark green paint.

6 Using the pale yellow paint from Step 1 and the fine paintbrush, paint leaf shapes on the cabbage stone. Again, this will look better if it is rough and not too neat.

7 Take the brown pebble and paint a few dots in darker brown paint (add a touch of black to your brown paint) to make it look like a potato.

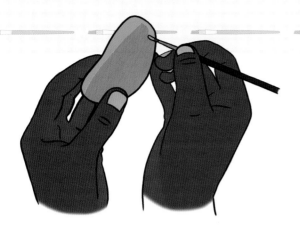

8 Now paint the sweetcorn. Add some white paint to your brown paint to make pale brown and then use this to paint all over the sweetcorn pebble. Leave to dry. Using green paint (add a little yellow paint to make it lime green) paint along either side of the stone to look like leaves. Leave to dry.

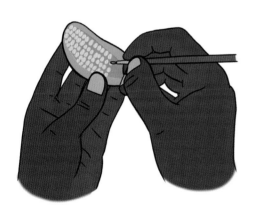

9 Using yellow paint, paint long rows of small brushstrokes on the brown section to look like corn kernels. These look even better if they are a bit patchy so don't worry about them being neat. Leave to dry.

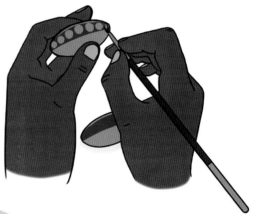

10 Paint the stones for the pea pods in green paint and leave to dry. Add a little black paint to the green paint to make it darker and paint a stripe along the stone. When this is dry, paint some round peas using the brighter green paint and leave to dry.

chapter 2

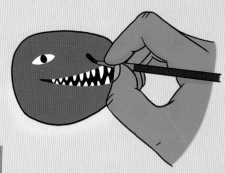

People and Creatures

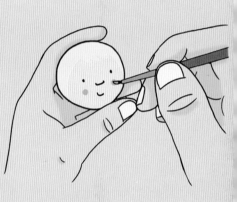

Googly-eyed monsters

Create these fun mini monsters and give them silly names.
You can keep one in your pocket like a lucky charm to give you
confidence when you're feeling nervous, or maybe give one to
a friend. Arrange them on a shelf in your bedroom to make eyes
at you when you're in bed—they are bound to make you smile!

You will need

Pebbles in any shape or size

Acrylic paint in a variety of fluorescent colors

Thick and fine paintbrushes

Plastic googly eyes

PVA/craft glue

Black and white paint

1 Paint each pebble a different color using a wide paintbrush. Paint one side first and leave to dry. Turn the pebble over and paint the other side. Leave to dry.

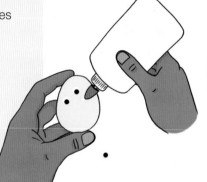

2 Glue some of the googly eyes onto each pebble. Remember, they are monsters so you can use as many or few as you like! Let the glue dry.

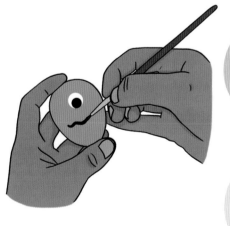

3 Using the black paint and a fine paintbrush, paint crazy mouths, eyelashes, and eyebrows in funny shapes onto your monsters.

4 When the black paint has dried, paint white teeth onto the mouths if you like.

Ghoulish ghosts

When your friends arrive for a Halloween party, these little ghosts could be peeping out of a window or standing on the table keeping watch over your Halloween food. You'll be surprised by how different their expressions can be depending on where you paint the eyes and mouths.

1 Using a medium paintbrush, paint the stone white. You may need to paint two coats (wait for it to dry in between coats) to get a nice even coverage. Paint the whole stone, front and back.

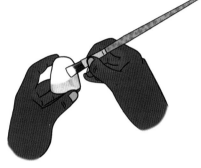

You will need
....

Flattish stones in different shapes and sizes

Acrylic white and black paints

Medium and fine paintbrushes

Black modeling clay

2 Take the fine paintbrush and paint two eyes and a spooky mouth onto the ghost. Don't worry too much about it being neat; they can just be splodges of black paint.

3 Using the same paintbrush, paint a jagged edge along the bottom of the ghost to look like raggedy fabric. Leave to dry.

4 Continue to paint your stones in the same way until you have a ghoulish group of ghosts ready for your Halloween celebrations. To stand them up, use a piece of modeling clay underneath each one to hold it in place.

Get ready to be SPOOKED!

Lovely ladybugs

Most ladybugs are red with black spots, but they come in other colors too. Some of them have lots of spots and some only a few, so find some in the garden or look at some pictures online and decide which ones you want to paint.

You will need

Round or oval stones

Acrylic paints in the following colors: red, yellow, orange, black, and white

Medium and fine paintbrushes

1 Take a stone and paint it with red, yellow, or orange paint. Don't worry too much about the underside of it, as it won't show.

2 Using the medium paintbrush, paint the head in black paint. Paint a line using the fine brush from the head to the bottom of the ladybug, adding a slight curve either side of the line where it meets the head.

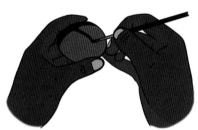

3 Paint black spots (small, large, or a mixture of the two) on one side of the ladybug, then on the other side, making your design symmetrical. You could use a Q-tip (cotton bud) instead of a paintbrush to make small round dots (see page 10).

4 Using white paint, paint two white eyes on the face; rather than painting them as dots try painting them as "comma" shapes to give your ladybug a bit of character. Mix a little red paint with some white to make pink and paint a small smiley mouth onto the face.

Dangerous dinosaurs

These dinos look pretty fierce, thanks to their sharp teeth! Paint them in different colors and add spots or zigzags for spines—whatever you fancy!

You will need

....

Flat, oval-shaped pebbles

Acrylic paint in the following colors: blue, green, yellow, white, black, and orange

Medium and fine paintbrushes

1 Paint the stones in blue, green, or orange, or any other color that you like. Paint one side of the stones first and leave to dry, then turn them over and paint the other side. Leave to dry again.

2 Using the fine paintbrush and black paint, paint the mouth onto the pebble in a triangle shape. Remember that you will need to paint the mouth on both sides and join the triangles up in the middle to make a big mouth which goes right around the pebble. Leave to dry.

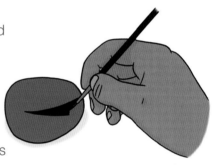

3 Paint small triangles in white paint around the edge of the mouth to look like teeth. Either make them all the same size or make some bigger than others. Leave to dry.

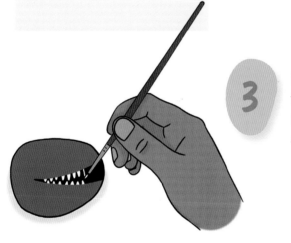

4 Using the white paint again, paint an eye onto both sides of your dinosaur and leave to dry.

ROOOOAAARR!

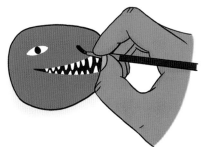

5 Paint a black dot in the middle of both eyes and a round nostril above the mouth on each side and leave to dry.

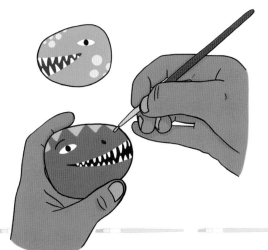

6 Decorate your dinosaur with spots or a jagged pattern along the top of the head using paint in a different color to the background. Mix your own colors if you like. You may need to paint one side, leave it to dry, and then paint the other side so that you do not smudge the wet paint.

Fun fish

You can find real fish in all kinds of amazing shapes and colors so look to the ocean for inspiration for this fun, fishy project. Find flat stones for the bodies, painting them in bright colors with different patterns on each one. Add smaller pebbles for tails. If you find a rectangular stone, you can make a whale too, complete with a water spout!

1 Sort out your stones, using the photograph as inspiration, so that you have a large rectangular stone for the whale and smaller roundish stones for the fish. Match tails to the whale and each of the fish and choose a triangular stone for the whale's water spout. Find three tiny pebbles, all slightly different sizes, for the bubbles.

2 Paint the whale's body and tail in gray (mix white and black paint, and the fish and their tails in turquoise, pale yellow, pale green, pale orange, and dark orange. You don't need to paint the back of the stones, but make sure you paint the edges so none of the surface of the pebbles can be seen. Leave to dry.

Make a splash...

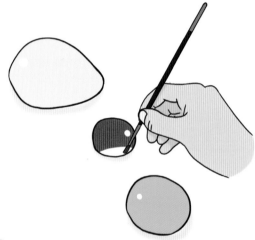

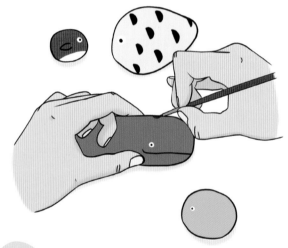

3 With white paint and a fine paintbrush, paint a small circle for an eye on each fish. Paint a white tummy on the dark orange fish.

4 Using a fine paintbrush and black paint, paint a small dot in the middle of the eye. Now, using the photograph as a guide, paint lines, triangles, D shapes, or scallops onto the fishes' bodies and leave to dry. Paint a long mouth onto the whale and a small black circle at the top for the blowhole.

5 Now take the painted tails and paint lines on them using black paint and a fine paintbrush, using the photograph as a guide.

6 Paint the pebble for the whale's spout with white paint. When it is dry, paint a few lines on it with gray paint.

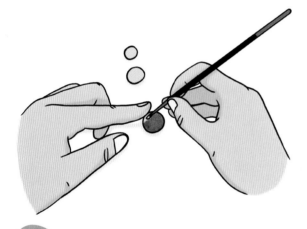

7 To make the bubbles, paint the three small stones in blue paint and leave to dry. Arrange the fish and the whale with their tails into an ocean scene. Add on the whale's spout and the fishes' bubbles. You could add in some natural rocks, shells, and green ribbons for seaweed.

Make your own people

Create crazy folk with these fun painted pebbles.
Paint heads, bodies, arms, legs, and feet and mix and
match them to make lots of different characters.
The only limit is your imagination.

You will need

Flat pebbles in various shapes
and sizes—think about what
works for heads, bodies, and
limbs

Acrylic paints in the following
colors: red, yellow, blue, green,
orange, black, and white

Mixing palette or white plate

Medium and fine paintbrushes

Black felt-tipped pen

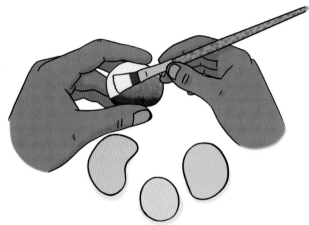

1 Take the pebbles that will work well for heads and
paint them in colors that you would like for the
faces—you don't have to stick to skin tones so mix
up whatever colors you like! Leave to dry.

2 Paint hair onto the heads in different
colors and hairstyles. Add beards
and mustaches to some of the men.
Leave to dry.

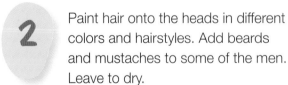

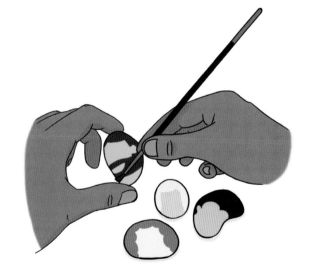

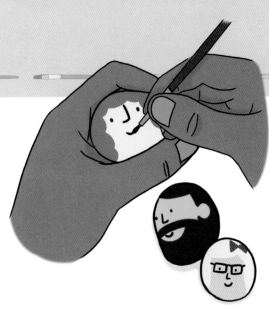

3 Using either the black felt-tipped pen or black paint and a fine paintbrush, draw or paint features onto the heads.

4 Choose pebbles for the bodies, arms, and legs and paint them all with a base color, using either the same color for all of them or different colors. Leave to dry.

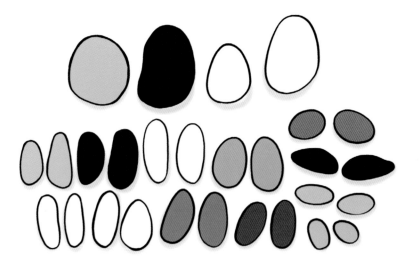

Mix and match head, bodies, and limbs!

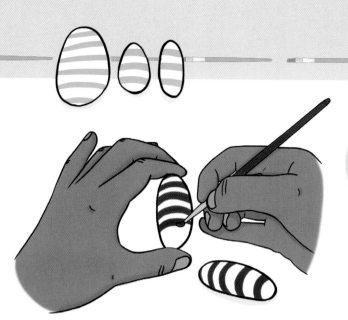

5 Paint or draw stripes and details on the bodies using any colors that you like. You can make these as detailed or as simple as you like.

6 Choose two small pebbles for each person and paint them to make shoes. When the paint is dry, draw laces or any details that you like on them with the felt-tipped pen.

Smiley faces

Why not make a whole family of these, or perhaps base them on your friends? Put them in secret places where people will come across them to make them smile back.

You will need

Round, flat pebbles

A selection of acrylic paints, including skin-colored tones, yellow, pink, and black

Mixing palette or white plate

Medium and fine paintbrushes

Pencil

Black and brown felt-tipped pens

1 Mix some paint in a skin color and paint the whole of one side of a pebble, painting around the edge as well so that none of the surface of the pebble can be seen. Leave to dry.

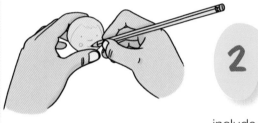

2 With a pencil, draw the hair, eyes, nose, mouth, round cheeks, and any other details that you would like to include, such as glasses or freckles.

3 Choose a hair color and paint the hair on your pebble with a medium paintbrush, painting around the edge as well. Leave to dry.

4 Using the felt-tipped pens, draw the eyes, nose, mouth, and glasses or freckles using either the black or brown pens. Leave the rosy cheeks as pencil outlines.

5 Using pale pink paint and a fine paintbrush, paint the rosy cheeks on and leave to dry. Paint on any bows or clips on the hair that you would like. Leave to dry.

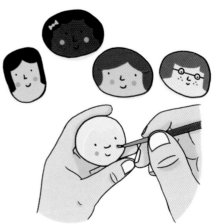

Pocket penguins

These adorable penguins look striking lined up on a shelf, especially if you make them in different sizes to create a whole family. Aside from paint, you will need a small amount of modeling clay for the feet.

You will need

Oval stones

Acrylic paints in the following colors: red, orange, yellow, black, and white

Medium and fine paintbrushes

Eggcup (optional)

Orange modeling clay

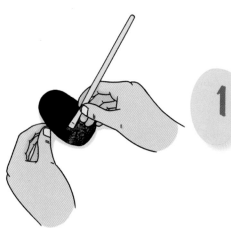

1 Paint the whole pebble black and leave to dry. Prop it up in an eggcup if you have one.

2 With the white paint, paint the tummy onto the penguin, using the photograph here as a guide.

3 Using white paint and the fine paintbrush, paint lines onto the sides of the penguin to look like wings and two dots for eyes. Leave to dry.

4 With black paint and the fine paintbrush, paint two black dots in the larger white dots for eyes.

A perfect PENGUIN family

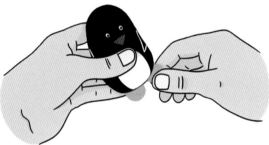

5 Using the orange paint and a fine paintbrush, paint a triangle under the eyes for a beak. Now paint a rough orange line at the top of the tummy, followed by a yellow one. These can be quite rough. Use a dry paintbrush to blend the two stripes together. Leave to dry.

6 Take two pieces of modeling clay and roll them into oval shapes. Join them together at one end and flatten them a little. Press the penguin onto them to make the flippers.

Zoo animals

There are lovely designs here to begin your very own zoo of friendly animals. Once you've got started, you can add even more. Looking at pictures of animal cartoon characters might give you some good ideas.

1 Paint one pebble white, one orange, one yellow, and two brown and leave to dry. Paint one side and leave to dry and then turn the pebbles over and paint the other sides.

2 To make the panda bear, take the white pebble and, using a fine paintbrush, paint two black ovals for the eyes, two ears, and a nose and mouth. When the paint is dry, paint two small white circles on the black eyes and leave to dry. Draw a small black dot using the fine liner in both eyes.

You will need

Round pebbles

Acrylic paints in the following colors: black, white, yellow, orange, and brown

Mixing palette or white plate

Medium and fine paintbrushes

Black fine liner

3 For the lion, paint a border of orange paint around the yellow pebble, making the edge a jagged shape. When the paint is dry, use the black fine liner to draw eyes, a nose and mouth, whiskers, and a few dots between the whiskers and the nose. Using the orange paint and a fine paintbrush, paint a stripe of orange paint above the nose and then paint the two ears. Leave to dry.

Animal MAGIC

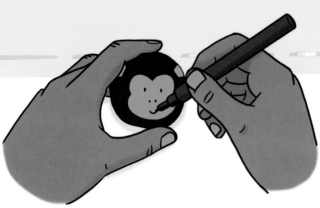

4 To make the monkey, mix some white paint with brown paint to make a light brown. Using the artwork above and the photograph on the previous page as a guide, paint a face onto one of the brown pebbles, then paint two ears. When the paint has dried, use the black fine liner to draw two eyes, two nostrils, and a smiley mouth.

5 For the bear, take the other brown pebble and, using the light brown paint, paint two ears. Paint an oval shape for the nose and two small eyes in white paint. Leave to dry. Draw the nose and mouth onto the nose shape and two black dots on the white eyes.

6 For the tiger, take the orange pebble and paint a white shape on the bottom of the face, as well as two dots for eyes. Mix a little white and orange paint together and paint a stripe from the top of the white shape to the top of the head. Then paint two ears. With black paint, paint stripes around the face, a line around each ear, and a nose and mouth. With a fine liner, draw whiskers, dots in the white eyes, and a few lines on the ears.

Swaddled babies

It's nice to have something to take care of and these adorable little babies are so easy to make that you can create lots of them for you and your friends. Paint the blankets in different colors and give their cute faces different expressions to create a whole nursery of babies.

You will need

Oval pebbles

Acrylic paints in the following colors: pale blue, pale pink, yellow, green, white, brown, and black

Mixing palette or small plate

Medium and fine paintbrushes

Q-tips (cotton buds) (optional)

Black fine liner

1 Mix a skin tone using your paints and paint a circle for the face on the top half of your pebble with the medium paintbrush.

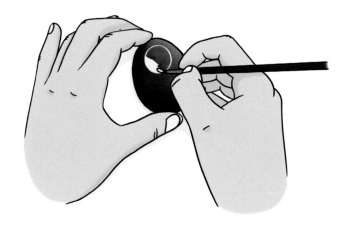

2 Paint the rest of the pebble in one of the other colors, ideally a pale pastel color, painting around the face neatly. Leave the front to dry before you turn it over and paint the back.

3 When the paint is completely dry, draw the eyes and mouth onto the face with the fine liner, then use the fine paintbrush to paint two rosy cheeks with pink paint.

4 Use the fine liner to draw some folds in the fabric. Don't worry about them being too neat. Add any extra details that you like, such as hair, ears, or a frilly collar around the neck.

Just too cute!

5 Paint polka dots all over the blanket, if you
like, using a fine paintbrush and a brighter
color than the one used for the blanket.
If you prefer you can use a Q-tip (cotton
bud) instead of a paintbrush to make round even
dots (see page 10). Use a clean Q-tip (cotton bud)
for each color you use. Leave to dry.

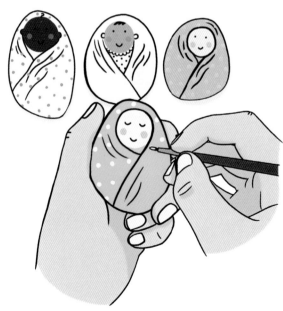

Enchanting elephants

Try to find three stones that are similar shapes but different sizes to create this cute elephant family. Why not paint their blankets in different colors to give each elephant its own personality, or look for even smaller stones to make tiny baby elephants?

You will need

3 largish, roughly rectangular stones, each bigger than the last, which will all stand up (you could always use a piece of modeling clay to help them balance)

Acrylic paint in the following colors: black, white, turquoise, pink, and yellow

Mixing palette or white plate

Medium and fine paintbrushes

1 Mix white and black paint together to make gray. Use it to paint all three stones with a medium paintbrush and leave them to dry. You won't need to paint the bottoms of the stones where they stand.

2 When the stones are completely dry, paint a rectangle to look like a blanket going over the back of each of the elephants using the turquoise paint. Leave to dry.

3 Paint a smaller rectangle using pink paint in the middle of the first one and leave to dry.

4 Using yellow paint and a fine paintbrush, paint small tassels along the bottom edge of the blanket and a swirly pattern and a couple of lines onto the pink rectangle. Do this on both sides of the elephant.

5 Add a little more black to your gray paint to make a darker gray color. Use a fine paintbrush to paint a tail, legs, a trunk, ears, and eyes onto each elephant. Turn them over and paint legs, an ear, and an eye on the other side.

6 Paint a few lines onto each leg and the trunk to look like wrinkles and two dots on the bottom of each leg for the toes.

Tip

With a collection of different-sized stones you can makes an impressive shelf decoration, with your elephant family all standing trunk to tail.

Delightful Dogs

These adorable pups are great fun to make and look so cute too. Paint them to look like your own dog or a pooch that you know or design your own hilarious hounds! Make kennels or dog beds out of cardboard boxes to keep them safe.

It's a **DOG'S** life!

You will need

Round stones for the body and head

Smaller flattish stones for the ears, paws, and tail

Fast-drying PVA/craft glue

Modeling clay

Acrylic paints in white, black, and brown

1 Sort out your stones so that you have a body, head, four legs, two, ears, and a tail for each dog. Try to match stones so that you have similar sized ears, front legs, and back legs for each dog and find a head that is a good size to go with the body.

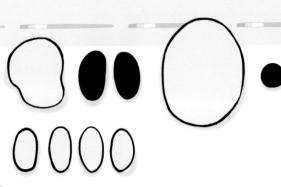

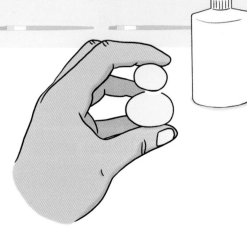

2 Paint the stones for the Dalmatian white apart from the ears and tail, which should be black. Paint all the stones for the gray dog and the brown dog in either gray or brown paint. You will need to paint both sides of the stones so paint one side first, leave to dry, and then turn them over and paint the other side. Leave them all to dry.

3 Glue the head in place on the body using the fast-drying glue. Hold it in place while the glue dries by supporting it on a piece of modeling clay. Leave to dry completely.

4 Glue the ears and tail in place, again holding in place with pieces of modeling clay until the glue has dried.

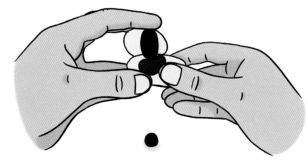

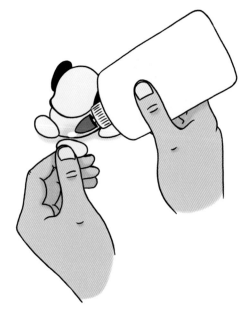

5 Now add the legs: glue two small stones to the front of the dog and two larger ones to the back. Hold in place with modeling clay if necessary until the glue is dry.

6 For the Dalmatian, paint a face on to the head using a fine paintbrush and black paint and add dots all over the head and body.

7 For the gray dog, mix a paler and a darker gray and paint a few rough brushstrokes onto each paw, the tail, and on the face. Paint eyes and a nose and small dots onto the face with black paint.

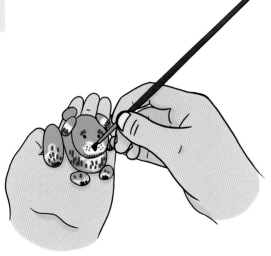

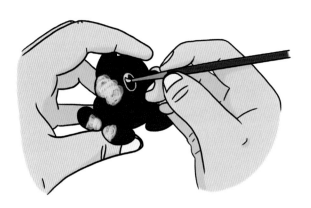

8 For the brown dog, mix white paint with brown paint to make a beige color and paint a patch for the eye and a few rough brushstrokes onto the paws, tail, and face. Paint a nose, a few dots around the nose, and two eyes using black paint.

chapter 3

Patterns and Shapes

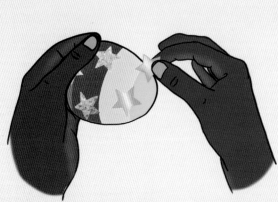

Simple patterns

Painting your stones in pretty colors and patterns is a lovely way to be creative, and they look striking grouped together. Here are some ideas to get you started, but you can create whatever designs you like.

You will need

Large pebbles in any shape

Acrylic paints in pretty pastel colors: yellow, green, blue, orange, and pink. Mix white paint into the colors to make the colors softer if you like.

Mixing palette or white plate

Thick and medium paintbrushes

1 Paint the pebbles in your chosen colors, using the thick paintbrush. Make sure that you paint all around the sides so that none of the pebble's surface can be seen.

2 When the base coat of paint has dried, choose another color of paint and paint some big spots onto one of the pebbles using the medium paintbrush.

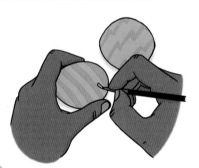

3 Take another pebble and paint stripes with another color of paint.

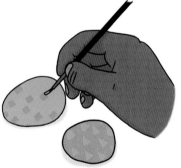

4 Paint squares or triangles on to the other pebbles or perhaps other patterns, such as zigzags.

PRETTY pastel pebbles!

Black and white flowers

Monochrome art—just using black and white—looks striking and sophisticated. This project uses 3D paint from a bottle so the pattern stands out from the pebble. It's a bit like using writing icing to decorate cakes! Use the photograph and artworks as a guide to begin with and then start to experiment with your own patterns.

You will need

Round, flat pebbles

Black and white acrylic paint

Thick paintbrush

Black and white 3D fabric paint or similar

Scrap paper

1 Paint the pebbles black or white. Don't worry too much about painting both sides of the pebbles, as you will only see the tops. Leave to dry.

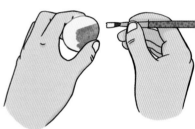

2 Take the black and white 3D paints and try them out on some scrap paper—practice making patterns with them. Try to squeeze the tube gently so that the paint does not come out too quickly. Keep a gentle pressure and the paint will come out evenly.

3 Paint simple flower shapes onto the painted pebbles, using the ones here as inspiration or create your own designs. If you are not happy with your design, simply wipe it off with a tissue and start again.

4 Add small dots around the flowers or in the centers for more decoration. Leave the pebbles to dry—read the instructions on your paint bottle for guidance, but this type of paint can often take at least 4 hours to dry completely.

MONOCHROME magic!

Love hearts

Look for some smooth, flat pebbles to make these pretty heart designs. They are perfect for Valentine's Day, or you could make them to give to your best friends. Why not paint hearts together as a fun party activity so that everyone can take one home?

1 Paint all of the pebbles in either white or in different shades of pink—you can make up your own pink colors by mixing red and white together or add white to your pink paint to make it paler. Leave to dry.

You will need

Flattish pebbles

Acrylic paints in white, red, and pink

Mixing palette or white plate

Medium and fine paintbrushes

Pencil (optional)

Q-tips (cotton buds) (optional)

2 Using the fine paintbrush, paint a white heart shape onto a pink painted pebble and leave to dry. Try reversing the colors so you have some white pebbles with pink hearts on. Each heart can be different to fit the shape of the pebble but you may want to draw it in pencil first to get a shape you really like.

3 Using red, a different shade of pink paint, or white paint, decorate the hearts with dots or little lines and leave to dry. You can use a Q-tip (cotton bud) instead of a paintbrush to make round even dots (see page 10). Use a clean Q-tip (cotton bud) for each color you use for the dots.

Noughts and crosses

Paint your pieces and then play your game! This set is ideal to take on journeys when you might get bored. Choose small pebbles in similar sizes, paint noughts and crosses on them, and keep them in a little bag with the grid painted on it so that you can play wherever you go.

You will need

12 flat pebbles

Pencil

Acrylic paints in green and blue

Fine paintbrush

Plain rectangular fabric bag, about 8 x 8 in. (20 x 20 cm), available from craft shops

Piece of scrap paper

Fabric paint in a tube with a small (tip) nozzle

1 Use a pencil to draw noughts on six pebbles and crosses on the other six.

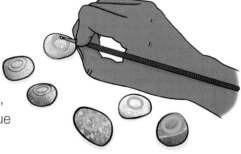

2 Using a fine paintbrush, paint the noughts in blue paint and leave to dry.

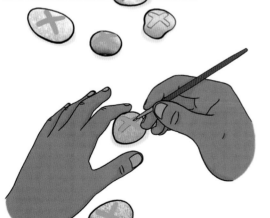

3 Paint the crosses in green paint and again leave to dry.

Can you get **THREE** in a row?

4 Place a piece of scrap paper inside the fabric bag. This will stop the paint soaking through to the other side of the bag. Using the fabric paint, paint two vertical lines and two horizontal lines on the bag to make the grid. You will not need a paintbrush for this—simply squeeze the paint out from its tip (nozzle). If you think you will find this difficult, use a ruler and pen to draw the lines before you paint over them. Leave to dry completely before you remove the scrap paper. Fabric paint can often take a couple of hours to fully dry.

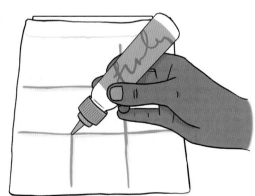

Glitter pebbles

These stylish, glittery stones would make lovely paperweight gifts for friends and family. You could even use some bigger stones for these—they would always be useful when trying to read a newspaper outside on a windy day!

You will need

Pencil

Round pebbles

Acrylic paints in the following colors: light blue, pale turquoise, dark blue, pink, gray, and white

Medium paintbrush

Scrap paper

Fast-drying PVA/craft glue

Gold glitter

Modeling clay (optional)

Pots or egg cups big enough to hold the pebbles upright (optional)

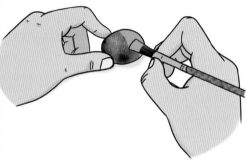

1 Draw a neat line in pencil around the middle of each pebble. Paint one half in one of the paler colors and leave to dry. If you place the pebble in a pot or egg cup, you can paint all the way round in one go.

2 Paint the other half of some of the pebbles in dark blue and leave to dry. Leave the others natural.

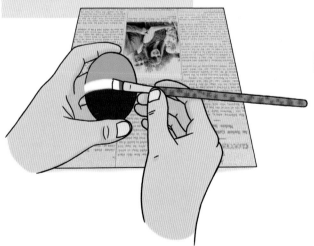

3 Lay some scrap paper over your table. For smaller pebbles, hold each end of the pebble between finger and thumb and paint a strip of fast-drying glue all the way around the middle between the two colors. For a bigger pebble, support each end on a lump of modeling clay and turn it as you paint the line of glue.

4 Still holding the pebble, sprinkle glitter over the glue, turning it until it is all covered. Shake it a little to remove any excess glitter. Leave the pebbles to dry standing in pots or egg cups that don't touch the glue. Fold up the scrap paper with the glitter inside and pour the extra glitter back into the pot so that it can be used again.

Dotty patterns

You don't always need paintbrushes to paint with. These dotty patterns are made using Q-tips dipped into colored paint to get even-sized round dots. Cover the whole surface of the stone with dots or perhaps make a wavy trail of them from one side to the other.

You will need

....

Round pebbles

Acrylic paints in the following colors: green, blue, orange, yellow, white, and black

Paintbrush for mixing paints

Mixing palette or white plate

Q-tips (cotton buds)

 1 Mix up a few shades of green paint, adding some white or yellow to your green paint.

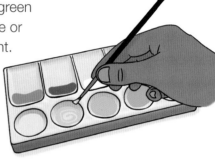

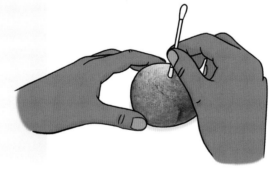

2 Take a Q-tip (cotton bud), dip the end into one of the colors, and make a dot on the pebble.

3 Take another Q-tip (cotton bud), dip it into a different shade of green, and make dots around the first dot you made on the pebble.

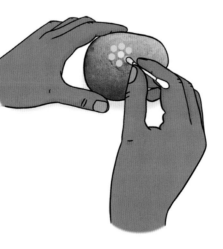

Variation
You could paint your pebbles first to make them even more colorful and then add a contrasting dotty color on top.

4 Continue to do this to make a pattern of dots in various shades of green or try making random dots in all the different colors.

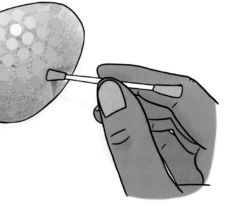

Go completely DOTTY!

Stars and stripes

Using stickers is a great way of making patterns on pebbles. Stick star-shaped stickers onto pebbles, paint over them, then peel the stickers off to reveal neat star shapes underneath. Of course, you can use other shaped stickers as well!

You will need

Smooth round pebbles

Small star stickers

Pencil

Acrylic paints in pink, orange, yellow, green, and turquoise

Mixing palette or white plate

Medium paintbrush

1 The smoother the pebble, the better this will work because the paint won't creep underneath the sticker. Stick some star stickers onto a pebble and press them down firmly. Use four or five stars for each pebble.

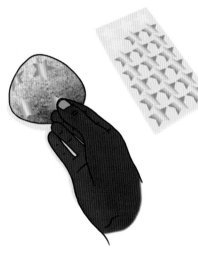

2 Using the pencil, draw lines across the pebble to make a few even stripes.

3 Paint each stripe a different color, mixing some white paint with the pink to make a paler pink. Let each stripe dry before you paint the next one.

STAR-SPANGLED stones

4 Leave the painted stripes to dry completely. Carefully peel the star stickers off the pebble to reveal the star shapes.

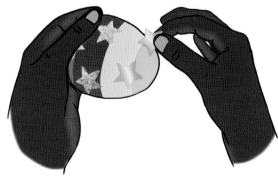

Rocky rainbow

Maybe you will find out what's at the end of the rainbow with this brightly painted pebble project. Choose pebbles in similar sizes and arrange them in a rainbow shape, painting each stripe in a different color. Paint two large stones to look like clouds to go at the ends.

1 Lay a few of the pebbles, about five, in a semicircle shape and paint them all purple on one side and let them dry.

You will need

....

Lots of small pebbles in similar sizes

Two large stones for the clouds

Medium paintbrush

Acrylic paints in the following colors: purple, turquoise, bright green, yellow, orange, red, and white

Pencil (optional)

Black felt-tipped pen

2 Lay the purple pebbles in a semicircle again and arrange some more pebbles in a larger semicircle around these. Six pebbles were used here, but that you may need more or less depending on the size and shape of your pebbles.

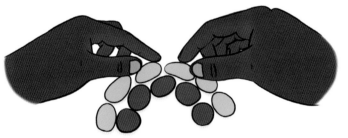

3 Paint these pebbles turquoise on one side, leave them to dry, and then place them around the purple ones.

A rainbow BRIGHTENS your day

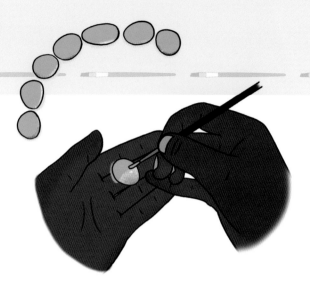

4 Arrange another row of pebbles around the turquoise ones (you'll need about eight). Paint them all green as before and when dry, place them around the turquoise pebbles.

5 Continue to make stripes of color in the same way, using the yellow, orange, and red paints. Paint roughly 10 pebbles yellow, 12 pebbles orange, and 13 pebbles red. You can add or take away pebbles as you need them.

6 When all the pebbles have been painted on one side, let them dry and then turn them all over and paint the other sides. Make sure you wash and dry your brush really well between colors. Paint the two large stones in white and leave to dry.

7 Using turquoise paint mixed with a little white, paint a scallop shape around the edge of the stones so that the white part looks like a cloud. You may find it easier to draw on the cloud shape with pencil first.

8 When the paint is dry, use the felt-tipped pen to draw a black line around each cloud. Position these clouds at the base of the rainbow.

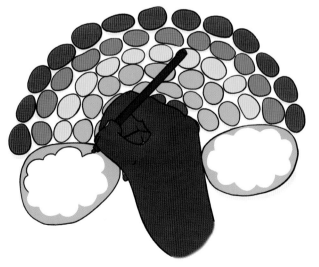

❗ Warning: Small pebbles could be a choking hazard. Always keep them out of the reach of young children.

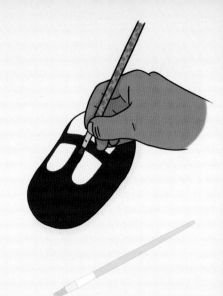

chapter 4

Home and Garden

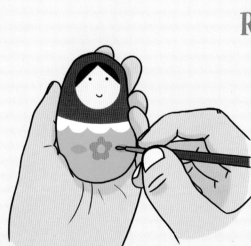

Lovely leaves

Get inspiration for these lovely, leafy pebbles by looking for different types of leaves the next time you're out for a walk—you'll be amazed at all the different shapes and colors! We have painted green leaves, but in the fall (autumn) you could use the colors of fallen leaves.

You will need

Flat, smooth stones in a variety of different shapes

Acrylic paint in the following colors: pink, yellow, red, orange, green, and white

Mixing palette or white plate

Medium and fine paintbrushes

Leaves you have collected

Pencil

1 Using the colored paints, paint the stones and leave to dry. Don't worry too much about painting both sides of them, as only the tops will show.

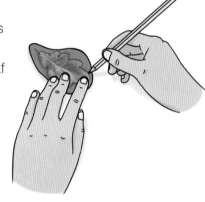

2 Either hold one of your leaves on a stone and draw round it with a pencil or observe a leaf closely and draw your own shape onto the stone. Draw different leaves on each of your stones.

3 Paint inside the drawn leaf shapes with green paint. Mix different shades of green, adding white and yellow paints to get different shades to match the leaves. Leave them to dry.

4 Mix the green paint with some white to make it paler. Using the fine paintbrush, paint the veins onto the leaves. Look carefully at each of the leaves you have used to work out the patterns of the veins.

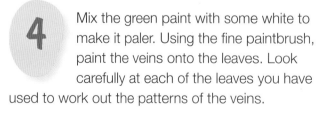

Cacti pebbles

Cacti grow in all sorts of wonderful shapes and sizes—some even look like pebbles, even though they are plants! Use tiny flowerpots and cacti-shaped pebbles to create a cactus garden of your own. Feel free to alter the patterns on the plants as you wish and have fun experimenting with different shades of green.

You will need

Medium-sized pebbles (some flat, some round) and a few very small flat pebbles to stick onto the larger ones

Acrylic paint in the following colors: green, white, and yellow

Mixing palette or white plate

Thick and fine paintbrushes

Egg cups (optional)

Mini pots—we used 1 in. (3 cm) and 1½ in. (4 cm) wide pots

Brown modeling clay

Fast-drying PVA/craft glue

1 Using the thick paintbrush, paint all the pebbles with green paint. Make different shades by adding white or yellow paint to the green paint so that each pebble looks a bit different. Leave them all to dry completely. If you have any egg cups, it can be handy to pop the painted pebbles into them to dry.

2 Using the fine paintbrush, paint vertical lines from the top to the bottom of one of the green pebbles with white or yellow paint. Don't worry too much about them being straight. Leave to dry.

Cute cacti—without the PRICKLES!

3 Using the fine paintbrush again, paint little crosses down the lines that you painted in Step 2, and paint little crosses on some of the other green pebbles to look like spikes. Leave to dry.

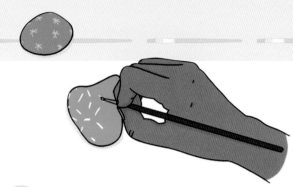

4 Again using the fine paintbrush and either the white or yellow paint, paint little lines or spots on the remaining green pebbles and leave to dry.

5 Glue very tiny pebbles onto either side of one of the larger ones so that they look like the arms of the cactus. Hold them in place while the glue dries by supporting them on pieces of modeling clay. Once the glue is dry, you could add another even smaller pebble to one of the ones you have glued on, but remember that the glue won't be strong enough to hold heavy pebbles. Leave to dry completely.

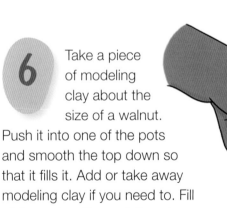

6 Take a piece of modeling clay about the size of a walnut. Push it into one of the pots and smooth the top down so that it fills it. Add or take away modeling clay if you need to. Fill all the pots with modeling clay.

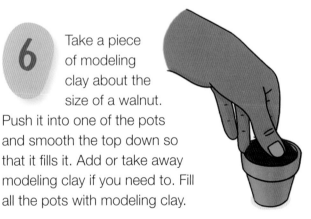

7 Push the bottom of the pebbles into the modeling clay so that they are firmly held in place and continue until all the pebble cacti are in the pots.

Dream houses

Create a village of pretty houses using pastel colors and different-sized stones. Look for flat-bottomed stones so that the houses stand up on their own, but if they are a bit unbalanced use modeling clay to keep them upright. Use your imagination to make each house look different.

1 Mix white paint into your paint colors to make pale pink, pale orange, pale blue, pale green, pale yellow, and pale gray. Paint the stones in an assortment of pastel colors from the bottom up—you need to cover about two-thirds of the stone but you don't need to paint the base. Leave to dry.

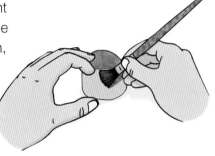

You will need

Stones in various sizes, with flattish bottoms so that they stand up

Acrylic paints in the following colors: red, orange, blue, yellow, black, and white

Mixing palette or white plate

Medium and fine paintbrushes

Black felt-tipped pen

Modeling clay (optional)

2 Mix a dark gray color by adding a little white paint to black paint. Paint the roofs on the stones. You can either paint the roof with a straight edge or with a scalloped edge. Leave to dry.

Tip
Paint trees onto cardboard, cut them out, and use modeling clay to stand them up around your houses.

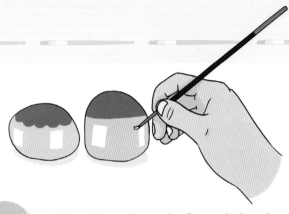

3 With white paint and a fine paintbrush, paint two rectangles onto the stones for windows.

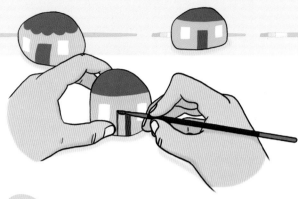

4 Using a darker color (red, dark green, blue, or brown), paint a rectangle for the door between the window rectangles.

5 When the paint is completely dry, use a black felt-tipped pen to draw lines around the windows, a small sill, and a cross to create the windowpanes.

6 Draw a line around the door in the same way, adding panels and a door handle if you like.

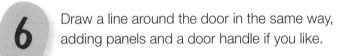

7 Draw lines, tiles, or little scallops on the roofs, again using the felt-tipped pen. Use modeling clay to keep the houses upright and stable, if necessary.

A village of cozy cottages

Cute cars

What kind of car-shaped stones can you find? Perhaps a cute Volkswagen Beetle or maybe a sleek Ferrari. You could even try recreating your own family's car and then give it as a present.

You will need

Large stones in car shapes

Acrylic paint in the following colors: green, blue, turquoise, black, white, yellow, and red.

Thick, medium, and fine paintbrushes

Pencil

Varnish

Tip

You'll need stones that are flat underneath, with good smooth curves over the top.

1 Using the thick paintbrush, paint the rock in one of the colors listed—or a different color of your choice. Don't worry too much about the underside of it as this will not show. Leave to dry.

2 Using the medium paintbrush and black paint, paint two circles for wheels on either side of your car. Leave to dry.

3 Mix black and white paint together to make gray for the windows. Draw them with a pencil and then use the medium paintbrush to fill them in.

4 Using the fine paintbrush, paint smaller circles of gray in the middle of the tires and leave to dry.

5 Again using the fine paintbrush, paint two headlights on the front of the car in yellow paint. You may need to use two coats of paint so that the car color does not show through. You could add brake lights in red.

6 Add some extra details to your car. You can paint a radiator at the front of the car by painting a black rectangle (again drawing it in place with a pencil if you like) and then adding some gray stripes across it. Add short black lines for the door handles.

7 To make the cars tougher, you can paint them with varnish or a layer of diluted PVA glue to prevent the paint chipping (see techniques on page 8).

Pretty flowers

This lovely project is very easy to make and you can have fun arranging the painted stones when they are finished. You can either put together simple two-color flowers or mix the petal colors for an extra bright display.

You will need

Medium-sized round pebbles for the flower centers

Lots of small round or oval pebbles for the petals and leaves

Acrylic paints in the following colors: orange, red, yellow, green, purple, white, and pink

Mixing palette and white plate

Medium and fine paintbrushes

1 Mix a little white into some yellow paint and paint the larger pebbles. Leave to dry.

2 Using a fine paintbrush, paint little dots in a darker yellow color (use yellow paint without white added) all over the painted pebbles.

3 Take about nine small pebbles (or as few or as many as you like) and paint them all in one of the colors— remember to paint both sides. Continue to paint groups of pebbles in the same colors, adding white paint to the red to make pink.

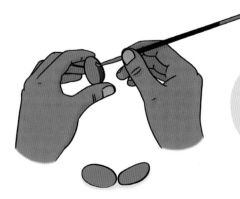

4 Paint a few pebbles green to use as stalks and leaves. Leave them all to dry before playing with them.

Gorgeous gifts

You can use any shaped stones for this project. Why not use them as place settings for a birthday party? Simply paint or write each person's name on a painted stone gift so that everyone knows where to sit.

You will need

....

Large stones

Acrylic paints in the following colors: yellow, pink, green, blue, and white

Mixing palette or white plate

Large and medium paintbrushes

Q-tips (cotton buds) (optional)

1 Mix up some pretty pastel colors and paint the stones all over in yellow, pink, pale green, or pale blue and leave to dry.

2 Using a medium paintbrush and a different color to the background, paint a cross on each stone to look like ribbon. When the cross is dry, turn the stones over and continue the ribbons from one side to the other on the underneath so there are no gaps. Leave to dry.

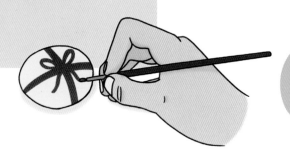

3 Paint a large bow on some of the stones using the same colored paint as the ribbon.

4 To paint a pompom decoration, paint rough lines from the middle of the ribbon cross about 1–1½ in. (2.5–3 cm) long in all the paint colors. It doesn't matter if the colors mix a bit.

5 Paint large or small spots on each stone to look like spotty wrapping paper. You can use a Q-tip (cotton bud) instead of a paintbrush to make small round even dots (see page 10). Use a clean Q-tip (cotton bud) for each color you use for the dots. Leave to dry.

Small parcels of fun

Baby shoes

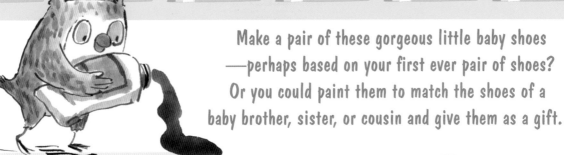

Make a pair of these gorgeous little baby shoes
—perhaps based on your first ever pair of shoes?
Or you could paint them to match the shoes of a
baby brother, sister, or cousin and give them as a gift.

You will need

2 shoe-shaped stones (they don't need to be exactly shoe-shaped or the same shape as each other as once they are painted they will look much more like shoes!)

Acrylic paints in the following colors: white, yellow, red, and brown

Mixing palette or white plate

Medium paintbrush

Pencil

Black fine liner

1 Paint the top of both of the stones with very pale yellow paint (mix a little yellow paint with white paint to make this) and leave to dry.

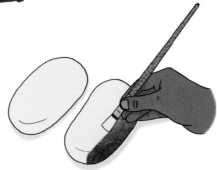

2 Use pencil to draw the shape of the shoes with a T-bar strap across them. Now paint inside the lines with red paint. Leave to dry.

3 Mix up a light brown colour by adding some white to the brown. Turn the stones over and paint the soles onto them, making the edge as neat as you can. Leave to dry.

4 Using yellow paint, paint a small, round button onto both shoes and leave to dry.

| 5 | Using the fine liner, draw stitching around the strap and the T-bar and two small dots on each button. |

| 6 | Draw a simple flower shape onto the front of both shoes and two lines around the soles to finish them off. |

Russian dolls

Russian dolls come in families with each one smaller than the next. Although, unlike traditional Russian dolls, these won't fit inside one another, they look brilliant standing in a row. Find stones that go from quite big to tiny, and then paint them all with the same hair and facial features so they look like a family.

You will need

5 stones in a similar shape from large to small

Pencil

Medium and fine paintbrushes

Acrylic paint in the following colors: red, turquoise, pink, yellow, orange, green, white, black, and lilac ·

Mixing palette or white plate

Egg cups or small pots (optional)

Black felt-tipped pen (optional)

Modeling clay (optional)

1 Using the pencil, draw a line around the middle of one of the stones.

2 Using the medium paintbrush, paint the top half of the stone with red paint and leave to dry. Paint the front and back—placing the stones in an egg cup or small pot, if you have them, can help.

3 Again using the medium paintbrush, paint the bottom half of the stone with one of the colored paints and leave to dry.

Tip
Finding pebbles of different sizes is more important than having five in exactly the same shape. Once the pebbles are painted, the shapes won't look as obvious.

Set them up from BIG to SMALL

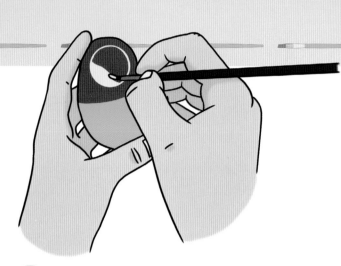

4 Mix some of the pink paint with the white to make the color for the face. Add a little yellow to make a peach color. Using the fine paintbrush, paint a circle on the top half of the stone for the face and leave to dry.

5 Again using the fine paintbrush, paint the scallop shape around the middle of the body with white paint.

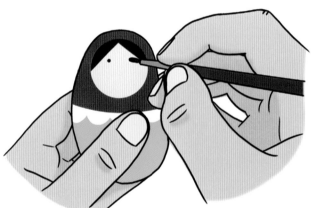

6 Using black paint, paint the hair, two small eyes, and a smiley mouth on the face. The eyes and mouth can be drawn on with a black pen if you prefer.

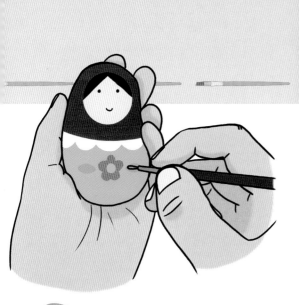

7 Paint a flower shape onto the bottom half of the body using one of the other colors. Drawing it with a pencil first can make it easier. Paint two small leaves with green paint on either side of the flower.

8 Add small pink cheeks to the face using pink paint mixed with a little white. Paint the rest of the dolls in the same way using the other colors of paint. Arrange them in size order. You may need some modeling clay to help them stand up.

PILLGWENLLY
01-08-18

Index

Suppliers

US

A C Moore
www.acmoore.com

Create For Less
www.createforless.com

Hobby Lobby
www.hobbylobby.com

Michaels
www.michaels.com

UK

Early Learning Centre
www.elc.co.uk

Homecrafts Direct
www.homecrafts.co.uk

Hobbycraft
www.hobbycraft.co.uk

Acknowledgments

I thoroughly enjoyed making the projects for this book but could not have done it without the following lovely people:

Debbie Patterson for the fantastic photography, fun shoots, and endless creativity. Clare Sayer and Dawn Bates at Cico for such supportive guidance, editing, and advice, Rachel Boulton for such clear and concise illustrations and Alison Fenton for the great design. And Cindy Richards, who trusted me to paint lots of pebbles and commissioned the book in the first place. Thank you all so much.

Thanks and heaps of love to Gracie and Betty for endless ideas, inspiration, and fantastic painting skills. And to Laurie for enthusiastic encouragement throughout.